I0109184

~Contents~

MARGOT HOJELL

THE INTERWOVEN BODIES
OF THE
COSMIC UNCONSCIOUS

Part I.

Spell Heaven

Nature produces (great) products, Don't
it
      Organic

A child who knows how to Spell
           Heaven
Surely must be brilliant
Even if it's spelled for him
        Directly about his head
In blue paper with
             Black letters

Jimmy just wouldn't listen
      Standing by my Dad at my old
      house,
          By the clearing
              In the woods
Closer to the clearing than me
But he still don't hear me-

He'll respond to the heaven above him
But won't even hear my Earthly voice
Won't even answer me

Still won't respond to my words
      Don't you hear them?
Do you speak on a slightly higher
frequency
         Level than me
Do you know who

Am I a stranger?
    Am I stronger?
        Why do you, so smart (so
        brilliant)
            Won't communicate
            with me
                In this lifetime
                Is it something/
                I've done/in the
                past?

You speak spiritfully low, praise
        You don't listen
Why is it that you speak to me
            Through these soul words
                Solely through poetry

But you won't speak to me on Earth-time
        On Earth, in Real Life
This one is dedicated to someone whose
        probably not in the audience
Who listens to my Poems?

You spell heaven
        I can speak of it
            You   spell
            I   speak
            You / don't answer me
            So how/do I know you're
            listening?

My mind's still not in the right place,
        Just yet
When will it be?

When we communicate in real terms
I'm still looking at you in the wrong
      Way
What about the
           Write place
I need the right space
My eyes not in the right place
      Still looking below where I have
          to

I must do/like you do,
      But in my own way
      Look over my head
      To spell heaven.

I had this
      Vivacious
      Dream about you.
You were
      Alive
      Healthy
      And
      Well.
You're hair was
      Growing
And you were
      Flourishing
Unlike the dream
      I had before
          Of you.
God bless you
You said you
      Saw me
          Online
And you decided to
      Call me.
Well I love you
      Well now I know what you
really look like
You treated me
      Well
You looked me
In the
      Eyes
          Jarringly
Gut-wrenching
          -ly
      Good

And I looked back
    And all I saw
        Was a guy staring
            Back at me
What do I
    Want?

I know you're going
        To Poland
        But so soon?
    What have I
        done,
and what do I
    do?
This isn't
    About you
    He/she says
I need to
    Rest in my
        Grave
And she tumbled
    Back to
        Sleep.

You sleep like
A Lamb
Even when you
Don't want to
Even when you don't have to
Even when you
Have other things
To do
You sleep like a
Lamb
Through the fortress
Of night
Tucked in
But not tied down
To the bed you're
Sleeping
In
You sleep like a
Lamb
Through the
Fortress of night
Not even fire-
Breathing dragons
Could keep you tied down
Nor sleeping
Princesses
Could wake you
Up/ or keep you tied/down
Do you

Sleep like a Lamb
All through the night
Through
Fortress(es) of
      Light?

I do,
      I Do.

Do you waste spaces
In potentially filled notebooks
(To) Trade them in for
Time and Space

Travel in your mind, (headed off/ to far
and distance places when you
Sleep?
Ooh, you know I do, I Do

I feel...

I feel encapsulated
      Traded me in for something
        You didn't
          Like
How can I stop it from happening
      Heaven's been put before us
        Will you take it
          And will I listen?
I feel encapsulated
      Lined up
      Like every time we talk
      I have to prove myself
      My worthiness to you
Tired of feeling illegitimate
      Next to you
When will my paranoia's
      Subside
      I hide all your secrets
      So well
What do I do with them
      Once you're—
I feel empowered to do the right
      Thing
      So I write this all down

      love.

Scratching, Clawing

Happy when I write in the chosen ending
    Where I stay in the shower a little
    While longer
Happy when I get out and my angry
    Uncle isn't clawing at the circular
    Bathroom window, pissed that I'm
Not ready
Happy when my family has given me
    Enough space and time to make
    My own decisions
        Decisions to decide to
        disagree
        With the populace
Happy to be me and suffer my own
    Fate not bending over backwords
        To hand my mother her own
            Life in a silver plate
Happy to write out the scratching
    Pigeons, cats clawing their way
    out of
        Boxes with horses giving
        the women
            Blood, transfusions
                And no I don't
                feel sorry,
                    Bad for
                    you.
You're just a pretty girl stuck
    In a bad relationship
        With someone that could
        make
            Me happy.

And when I go to Germany,
 This time I know better
 Not to leave my CD's
  On the
    Bus.
    I won't even
 Bring them
  With me.

And boy, if she kisses you where it hurts
 Will I feel Anything, at all?
    Better/When it's/
  Over?
And this time the lady in the water
 is me
   taking a shower

And this time the family doesn't
 Come
They wait
   For me
They give me, no need
To search for a savior
  Disguised as a martyr
   Who tells me "Don't bow
    Down to your
    mothers
     Every whim."

And I'd trust you, it's just
 That
A cool breeze teases my shoulders
  And laughs at the face of
   Love

In the direction
Of something
Better.

It wasn't all sad...

It wasn't all sad,
In fact,
He was there for her The day
He found out his body
Went missing
(He was there)
Standing by her Side
(To pull her Along)
(By Pulling across the Sun)
To Pull her along
Pulling her Along
To Pull Along the Sun
And drape it Across the horizon
The day of his funeral/For her
And Frankly,
The only bad thing about his?
Life was his untimely
Death
Everything else I've found out about him
is/they are
Positive and Rewarding
Things
Helping us along the way

Positive things about
        His life
This is not merely
        A boy/and his Death

It's celebrating the life (and times?)
            Of a boy
    Who happened to live an
            untimely
                Life
    It's about a boy
            Who (was about to suffer?)
                Who happened to
                suffer
                        An untimely
                        Death.

The San Fernando Valley

I'd take him over hills
      and high mountains
Over rich vivid orchids
      Each planted a perfect and
      Equal distance from one
          Another

And when he takes pictures,
      He moves mountains
He shifts continents
      And his finger, snapping
        The lens
Makes the sun's reflection
      Cry over the ocean.

Thinking of You

Alarm clock with planetary
   rings around it
It's thinking of me
    Giving me time to
      Dream in my sleep
Allowing me/ to think of
          You.

Alarm clock with pleasure
planetary
Rings around you
Is thinking of me
Giving me time to
Dream in my sleep
Allowing me (time)
To think of you

Alarm clock with planetary
Rings around it
Thinking of me
Giving me time
To dream in my sleep
Allowing me time
To think of you

Dream clock/Alarm clock
With planetary rings around it
Thinking of me
Giving me time
To Dream in my sleep
Allowing me time
To think of you.

The alarm clock hasn't forgotten
About me
It's waiting for
Whenever I'm ready
To reward me

Part II.

Logic's Eyes

Everything all of a sudden Seems
very divided
Her mother told her
I'd fall in love
with her personality
She was right
I feel it's so wrong
You don't see The
        repercussions
You and your friend(s)
want to take me To Louisiana
I am hesitant To go

I have to sign Papers
And I feel the Camera's closing In on us.
Church pews,
        School rooms
But it's at no
Expense to you
Nothing can be
Taken away from
        You
You just do what you
        Choose

Age separates us
A few years is
    A lot
Maybe in our
Past lives we were
    Lovers
Now I can hardly
    Look at you that
        Way
'cuz I know the hate it brings
I have my career
    On the
Line
    And know that it
        Just ain't
            Right.

Her mother told her
    I'd fall in love
        With her personality

And I knew she was
    Right
But that doesn't
    Save me from
    Age gaps-
        Multi-racial
        Barriers
        Not to mention
            Our gender
                Is the same
It feels taboo for
    Me/ It feels too far removed for
me (from me?)

But feels so real-
        Natural to her
I know it can
        Never happen
                Again in real life
At least not in
        Mine

I used to love her
        Unquestioningly
        In another life,
                Another/time
But (k)now I see
        Through logic's
        Eyes and I
                Cry (for what
        Could've been?)
                for what just ain't right?

Time's Sacred

I had this dream last night
That you were in the kitchen making a
Sunday
But it was a Saturday.

I had this dream last night
About this hike
A long
        S----T---R---E---T---C---H---
And along the stretch there was a path…

!

P

    U
    D

  N

A

P

    U

      D
      N

    A

P

U
W   T.
  I   I

    N

    .   D

 .   I

  P.   N

U   G.
           G
                  N
           I

        B
           M
        I

      L
        C

D   A Structures,
  N

The spring brook

The spring brook nearly drowned
                         Wy
Dreaming of me writing a poem
Driving backwards
Word missing words
                         Wy
Letters missing letters
                         Wy
Words missing letters
                         Why?
Filling in the missing letters in my head
                         Why?
Why did I choose why
        As the word to fill in with?
                When you(one?) sees a W
                and a Y,
                         They immediately see
                         and or think
                                Why?

23

Maybe I Should

Love bursting inside of me
Love bursting
Love burst a feeling inside of me
Love bursting
 Love bursting
        Love
                Love
                    Love

Maybe I should pay
        Attention when I
            Wake up
        The way I pay attention
            To myself in my
                Dream
Maybe I should pay attention
        When I
            Wake up
        The way I study my
            Dream material
Maybe I should vehemently
        Study my dream material
        The way I study my life
            When I wake up
Maybe I should dedicate
        My waking life to taking
            Notes
                Paying attention
                    To detail
                        Noting the
                            Abstract

Formulating it
　Into
　　　Reality
The way my dreams
　　Form
　　　　Pictures in my
　　　　　Mind
　　　　　　After I
　　　　　　　Wake up.

I don't need to

I don't need to
　Find/ every
　　　Moment/
　　　　　That don't
　　　　　　Matter/

Sad

"What are you doing
　sitting here
　　　still in school
　　　　Bags in tow?"

"Traveling,
　Always traveling.
Waiting,
　Always waiting,

I have been sitting on buses
        Since eight o'clock in the
                Morning might as well sit
                here and wait a little while
                        longer"
"Where are you coming from?"
"A place far away to visit
            Someone I think I know"

"What
        Did you guys do?"
"I guess we did
                Homework."

"Where do you
        Long
To be?"
        "I Long
to be
in one of your
Poems."
"O.K., Well I'll consider
        it."
"Well I've considered it, and I do
and I already did
And I will
And you already are
And you are
Now
So here you are
And there you go
Viola."

A "Marriage" Song-
A Different Kind of
Marriage.

      She   says
  "You're not alone" says   Spirit
     home from the Grave-A spirit
     from the Dead

A Spirit /coming back A Spirit /
             Coming back from
       the Ground
    coming home from a long /Journey/
               A Spirit
A spirit attaching   itself   Proud of me-
    To him   A Spirit
A spirit /?Alone in the Universe
Attaching itself
    To you
At peace in the   A Spirit, Awakened
    Light – surrounded by / Him /
You found me,
    Awakened
        A Spirit

Three Questions

I am or Am I not?
    Am I or Am I not?
        "To be or not to be, that is
        the
            Question"

I don't see a precious taking
    Care of
        Of the Self
    But many any? Other/People

    His brother was there
        And I said "hi" to Him-
    It doesn't seem to have a
        Timeslot
    I cannot seem to
        Place it

I need to seriously figure out
    What's going on
        So I know
            Whether or not
                I'm Doing the
                right
                    Thing

I've never felt energy
    Like I've done with this
        Full force

I would like to not-

Make Assumptions
I would like to not
Have assumptions made

I would like to not make
Assumption
I would like to not
Have assumption
Made.

BE MINDFULL

Not having a full mind,

But Having enough mind for your stuff
to matter (your?)
Having enough mind for stuff that
matters
Mind your matter
Having enough free-floating
Matter (Matter in your
mind)
Space in your mind

I'm on the phone
And in real life with the
Other-
I'm touching his hand
Physically
So maybe I'm physically
With this one guy
And Spiritually metaphysically

With the other(?)

But the guy I'm with,
        We're discussing opinions
                On what feels like
                Shakespeare lines
And he's disagreeing with Me
        And I Question,
                Ask myself,
                        Wonder
What am I supposed to be doing
        What/Am I/Supposed/to do?
Boy by my side in real life We're talking
        About-or we're disagreeing or
                Putting our rather
conflicting? Idea(l)(s?)
                        On the table

I am or I am not
Am I or am I not-discussing what that
"means"
        And his interpretation
                Differs, -From, Mine
So I'm on the phone with_
        And talking in real life
                (life?) to the-
                        other-
Touching his hand-
Lightly touch(ing) his hand
No lightning (plugs)(sparks) fall out

(drop?)
Lightly
Touching
His hand

No lightning
Plugs
Fall out
Gently
Touching
His hand-
No lightning
Plugs
Spark out

      But Disagreeing
            There's no lightening
                   Spark Plugs No spark
plugs BURSTING (serene)
            There's no beautiful, pristine
                 Just quiet, beautiful
                       Serene Sound
          Golden-ness
             (Goodness?)

There's no beautiful/?Goodness
        No warm surprises
"To be or not to be"... is that the
                          Question

There's no beautiful, pristine. serene
        Golden-ness
There's no beautiful, pristine

      Goodness
No warm Surprises

Fuck the Good/-ness
       Fuck the Fiction
Is that what you're asking?
I promise you'll never
       Leave my
       Mind
I don't think he was as
       Upset that I was flirting
With that guy

(They're having the
       Same exact Conversation
    They're having the Exact Same
       Conversation
I was

He said, "I don't like girls
       With nothing
         To talking about"

But see I was talking
       (I) just (not) (wasn't) to (Him
         Although the other guy that
           I was probably with

Don't you think the right
       Thing for me to do

Is what feels right/for me. ?

Call the other him
And show him
I have I wasn't to share
       With him

Have the/conversation
     I was meant to have
          With the other guy,
               And change the future
               And have it
               with
                    Him
Ask him, over the Phone, Three
               Questions.
Say, "Am I, Am I Not, or Am I just
                    Once?"

     Am I,?
          Am I not?
     Or am I just a Question?

             just a Question
       Am I,   not, (or)

What's going on in this Earthquake
     Of Sound and Noise

I have three Questions: ("Can I ask you a
               Question?")

Q: "Can I (and you?) ask you three
               Questions

     At once?"

     (you ?) (?)
Q: "I just Did" You just Did?
       A: (What?) Yea, Exactly
  Can I ask you three Questions
One at full force(?)

(c) at once)
One visible, Two Questionable,
        And three (invisible) Answerable
                With(out?) A Question
                That You
And three an answer that is
UnAnswerable
                That Answer your (my?) Question
                With the Answer of a
                        Question

I know/it all/goes back to
        "To be or not to be"

        (Question that is the)
That is the   Answer to my
        Question
That is the Question that is the Answer to
my
                        Question(s)
Overextending , stretching (out?)
        Reaching ourselves through states
        Of minds
And states and minds
Over continents and bodies of water
(over sound mind)

over extending, Reaching ourselves
        Through reaching, (leaning)
(backwords) (leaning towards) towards
                Eachother
Reaching Across Boundaries
        Limited By Physicality/-ie(s?)
(Boundaries)
Of Time, Space Continuum

Time, Space, Location

And Even sometimes reaching leaping
through physical boundaries
Leaning over Through Time and Space
Leaning leaping over Through Time

And Space.-
Leaning over space through
Time
Leaping Over Space through
Time
What's the missing link
Equivalent to this Question

I was wondering if you could
Ask these two Questions I wrote
With the third correct quote
Of a Question

The third part is the missing Link

The PROCESS of WRITING a SONG

(The Process of Healing)

(in?)
The Process of Building lyrics,
You write a New song

How do you/write/?a new?/
Song?

I have three Questions (-or-

Can I ask you three
          Questions?

She said I'm a genius
          But if I'm a genius
                    How come I let words
                    (now?) lag me
                              Instead of make
                              make(-ing) me
                    Making me fly
                              What does this
Can I   statement mean to
you
I have three Questions:
I am or Am I not?
          Am I or Am I not?
"To be or not to be"... that is the right
answer
                    to the Question

She's Obsessed
          Lost herself in Another/?Person

(Like)   herself

          God looking (at yourself

Good luck looking at yourself(.)
          God's looking at herself
                    Through a microscope

They sent for me,
          The Famous Poets
                    To deliver their

36

Message

Don't miss Me
For I Hear
Therefore I'm
            Here
                    Don't
Miss Me   For
I hear
Therefore I'm
        Here

Don't miss me
For I'm Here
        Therefore I
                Hear!
Don't miss me 'Fore I'm
        Here
                Therefore I
                        Hear
Two Different Voices
        I can't listen/to your

                Voice-Without seeing your
                Face
I can't listen to your Voice
Without seeing your/Face
        Face
If you have
Two Different Voices
Does that mean
        You have Two Different
                Faces
Space Rock Star
        Rock Star

Space Star
Space Rock Star
Rock Star
Rock Star
Space Star
Space Star
Space S   a   s   c
        P   ce   a   e

                        p
S   A   e   C
  P   ©   O
                R   K

S   A   E
  P   C   R   P R   C
                A   O   K
Portrait of my energy

C   L   E   R   Y
        A   L   M   C   A   Z

What sort of audience do you
        Like

I like things to make sense on
        An emotional level
                As oppose to a logical
                        Level

S   A   P
        P   C   S
                        E

38

Although small
    And still
        Empty,
Not [over?] crowded
Many? Multiple Beds
Crowded inside the larger house or
apartment
With the
Potential to
    Hold that
Many people-
Or? Even more
People inside

But this house
    A tree-house
        High up in the sky
Although small, sturdy
With just enough
    Room for
    You and me
        To fit inside
I can see my
Posters going
    Up on the
        Walls
And your
    bed fitting neatly inside
    Tucked away
    In the corner
    Our house
Although more
    Of a

Pretend play-
  House in the
  Mind,
  It fits us neatly
  Inside just
  Fine
Not quite as
Spacious
  As the
Apartments-

Houses with loads of bed? Rooms
In them
people in it
inside
That fit many multiple beds in them
But this one
  Will hold
Our one bed
  Just fine

Fuck you, Trip

Fuck you, Trip
I'm going on You
Before you can
 Go on it   get the chance to go]
And the collective unconscious-
          And could it hold
                It's contents-the quantity
[contents] of its
                    Origin
          And the collective unconscious
          Could it hold you
          Before you [contain] hold it.

Om

Om is sort of a
Trophy
          Sort of a
       Human type
       Thing
The triumph of being
          an om super
                activist
Is the benefit of getting to be
[To get] to being]
          A super human
                Being

D.C.

You, oh evil one
　　　Trying to fool Me

The children walking
　　　Around
　　　Pretending they're not
　　　　　Macaulay's
Beating me.
The Train Station
　　　Workers have a
　　　Mild taser system
　　　and they mildly
　　　taser the Children
Ask me if I'm a
　　　Mother
And I solemnly say
　　　"no"
I leave the Indian
Pregnant woman
　　　In D.C.
　　　By herself
　　　Olive
To fend for
　　　Herself
　　　To get lost for
　　　Herself
I don't wish her
　　　Good luck
　　　Or at least I [don't
　　　　　say it]
to her
But I leave,

Unannounced
Undeclared
I'm a Mother
Now
Will I ever
        Be?
Or will I just
        Be doomed to
        Walk this lonely
                Lovely planet

                Alone
                No one to
                Share it
With?

Workin' at an
    Alarm clock factory
    24 hours a day
Listening to people
    Tell me their
        Dreams
And (But?) you don't say
    A word
    You don't tell me
        Anything
I want you to tell
    Me
        All you're
    Deepest, darkest
        Secrets,
Feel bad for me
    Inside
           But instead
You just ask me
    What I learned
    From the
          Experience
Besides the Obvious,
    Never work
    24 hours a
        day
    Even for an
    Alarm clock
Factory

I'm not there
    For you
        To pave the

Path
To show you the
        Way
It's no longer
        You looking
                Out for me
It's me picking
        Up the pieces
To my broken
        Life

And slowly moving
On.

For me, a notebook
Speaks for it's
Writer.
This one says, "Help
Me."
"I'm a poor girl
who just graduated
college
and yearns for a
real job
in the city
something that
pays moderately
well
nothing too
serious.
A job that shows off
My real talent. Says:
            This girl can write!

This notebook says:
            Please help her!
                    She's so desperate
                        To write,
She'll start on the first
            Page on the page
                    Before the ones
                        With the lines
                                On it
And since she doesn't
            Have a job,
                    She makes good,
                        Full use

Of a notebook given
          To her/ by her
Aunt.
          She wants a job
                    So she can pay
For her own notebook
          So to speak.
                    Not that she doesn't
Appreciate this

          Book that's been
Given to her, God only
          Knows,
                    It helped to create
                              This poem,
But she wants a
          New job/
                    Life that speaks
          To her.
          Something that
                    Pleases her
                    New job please
Come out come out
          Wherever you are
And show
          Yourself
                    To me.

The Grad Student

There's a sense of building something
from the ground up
     (Like architecture?)
         When you sit at this Desk
A grad student's head/ is filled with
nothing/but Homework
     Look inside a Grad student's mind
         Sometimes they're more
forgetful,
             Just look at their
               Age
If they're really old they might be
driving
     Cars into
     Lakes.
Look at this desk
     Look at the abstract
         Thoughts that go into
             The students'
               Mind
The thoughts that wrinkle
     Con
        Form
          And
            Con
              Tract
What about the baby
     With the diaper
         That needs to be
            Changed?
I'll take care of that in a

Second,
      Just wait
         And see
Don't worry about
      Anything
         I'll take care of
            Everything
The undergrad
      Students mind
         Can fit a little
            More.

The abstract thoughts
      That form
         And wrinkle

         Inside the
            Grad student's
              Mind.
I wrote this when I was a
      Undergrad.

Your Favorite Idea

I am your favorite idea. I travel with
wind and sound. No matter how many
times you've put me to rest, You can
never fully put me down.
>Without you I cease to exist
>Write about you/ What about you?
>I'm abstract/ What you write about
>>What do you/write

about?
Illusive

>-Intrusive

Allusive
>Abstract
>Vivid when you let me be
>>You can never/fully/put me/
>>Down.

>>Write about me, write about me
>>Repeat…

Albert Einstein

Not Even Albert Einstein Cares
  About my mind
Even he is too busy Tryin' to pick
   Out girls that he can buy Pretty
   Dresses
I want my Love to buy me
  Pretty Dresses
  To notice my Physical
  Beauty
Like he and Albert Einstein
  Notice Everyone
  Else's

Albert Einstein rematerialized on
  My couch Last night
I walked towards him,
  Up to him
  To ask him
   A Question
But he was too busy
  Tryin' to pick out Girls
   With his Eyes
    To Buy
     Dresses
All I wanted was him to make enough
  Room
  For me to sit Down Beside him
   On the couch
So he could Answer Me a Few

Questions
I didn't care about standing
            In Front of him
                        So he could see me with His
                                    Eyes
I just want him/to make
            Enough room so I could sit
                        Next to him
            To (So he could) feel me
                        With My
                                    Mind!
But even feeling(s) are not
            Enough to keep a brilliant
            man

                        Distracted
                                    From his
                                    Wondering
                                                Eye(s?)
                        and his Lust for Physical
                                                Beauty

I dreamed I saw Albert
            Einstein Rematerialized
                        In my Dreams Last
                                    Night.
Not even Albert Einstein Cares
            About my mind.
I want Albert Einstein to
            Notice my Presence
The way he looks with his
            Eyes/ ?Trying to pick out/?girls

That he can buy/
Pretty
Dresses.

I want Albert Einstein
To feel/me with/his
Mind

But emotions(alone?)/ aren't enough/
To Hold a Relationship
Together. Not even for
Einstein
One must Appeal to the senses
Of both the Eyes and the/
Mind.

Nicaragua

I've been to Nicaragua
  Open windows on lofty floors
3 stories high in the air
and I'm looking down on a plain at
plants
  in the Desert

I've been to Nicaragua without planning
  It
Windows that go on from ceiling to
  Floor
I press my palms

In Nicaragua
I press my palms peering out? Windows
that
  Span from ceiling
     To
       Floor.
In Nicaragua
I press my palms on windows
  Peering out spans from Ceiling
       To
  Floor.
A window for once not keeping the
  Vision out
But bringing the beauty in
Although it's a window
  It's acknowledged as the outside
In Nicaragua
  I peer out windows that
  Draw me closer in to the outside

In Nicaragua
      The windows draw me closer
      Unifying me with the scenery,
Although the landscape parch,
One lush green Plant still expresses it's
own unique freedom
      To grow
It's not lonely- This one green thing is
enough
      To complete it's surroundings
Regardless of the parched landscape

      These plants are beyond the
Earthly
         Restrictions of silence or
science
They flourish regardless of their
environment

Instead of being protected

In Nicaragua
      The wind[ow] draws me closer
      Unifying me with the scenery
      Instead of needing to be protected

Regardless of the dry, parched landscape
      I appreciate the beauty of the
Earthly
      Brown substance

      I'm only scratching the surface

In Nicaragua
     I find myself suddenly sitting with
my Grandma in a restaurant
Although through previous logic I
wouldn't expect
     The food to be inadequate,
I have no memory- recollection of these
thoughts
     In this Place
The food is perfect
The fleshy fresh skin of oranges gently
lifted
Freshly orange slices
     More brilliant than I've ever
          Seen before in the flesh
A Plate is more than enough for this
     Feast of the eyes and soul
This orange makes all other oranges
     Seem foreign
This and only this is an orange
     Lively mangoes, riveting,
Ravishing
          The star of this vision
Fresh fruit is all I need to be given
Although it was one plate,
     At this place one is the only
          One
And the dish of delicious oranges stays
     Frozen in time
     Made pristine- serene by my mind
Never yet eaten
     Always freshly being brought to
     the table

This restaurant's got a door
    Deep wood
        Medium brown coloured
            Door-type-
            walls
    Bendable dressing room mobile?
      Wall

Each inch of the orange fleshy
    Freshly
        Gently peeled into sections
    Skin gently peeled
      For proof
        To prove
            To reveal…
The fleshy part of an orange.

"Just because I'm the new guy doesn't
mean I hold shit in," said the new guy
when he was accused of holding shit
in

And what about
Those drug
Addicts?
They show up
To a show
Like 10 years
Later and
Expect you
Not to notice
"That's because
Drug addicts
Have a
Warped
Perception
Of time,"
Said the
girl who
used to
hang out
with
drug addicts
to the slightly
older, middle-
aged man
She was in a
Supermarket

He was
Wondering
Why the
10-year-
Later person
Missed their
Chance/
(He was seeing
It more like
A missed
Chance)
She was
Seeing it
More like,

"drug addicts
Have a warped
Perception of
Time."
Hadn't shown
Up in so long

Suddenly the
girl finds
herself in
a house
there's a
strained
relationship
in the house

The man
Offers her
shoes
like cars
She tries
Them on
And accepts
Them
Even though
The shoe size
Is slightly
Off
But the shoe
Size she likes to wear
Doesn't have
Any shoes
For her
There's only
Only a purple
Hairbrush
In its place.
The woman
Talks to the
Slightly
Younger girl
Makes
Some state-
Me(a)nt about
Slightly older
Middle-aged
Men
And their
Unreliability.

They all convene on the patio
    Outside
        The one that's not
            Screened in
I feel many people
    Sitting down at
        Tables
I assume they might
    Be eating the way
        They're all sitting
            At tables
                On the open air
                    Patio

I used to live there
    But this is in the
        Era of a different
            Time
The waiter with the white
    Suite on looks
At me with his eerily
    White-pale
        Ghostly almost

            Transparent looking
              Face
It looks/feels like
    The 40's or maybe even
        The 20's
Regardless, the scene is
    From a long time
    Ago

It's like it's happening
                    Again
         In a different way
                    Spirits re-convening
                    And rematerializing
                         In a different
                              Way
A meeting of sorts
Where the spirit and the Earth
         World collide/convene
              Meet

It's like they were
         There but they
              Weren't there
                    All at the same
                         Time

He looks directly at me
         And smiles
              It seems he has
                    Something on his
                         Teeth
Braces of sorts

A procession
    But what
Kind of funeral
    Procession
        But there seems
            To be no body
            It's like
        They're looking
            For one
I run to get
    My gun
        That I didn't
            Know I had
        And even though
            I feel
Like it's not
    In the last
    Room
    I run by it
    Any way
    And see dusty
        Old, ancient
            Books
    Then I run
        To the other
        Room to
        Get my/look
    For my/a gun
    That I didn't
        Know I had
Maybe it's not
Mine
    But I had a

Picture
In my
Mind
Of where it
was

The boy

I watch the little boy
    But I have somewhere
        To go at 7:30 at night
We did not discuss
    When she would be
        Home,

The woman I assume to be
    His mother

I walk with the boy
    I assumed I was
        Babysitting

I take him to where he
    "lives"
    he climbs up open stair
        ladders
            more than one
                there must be
must've been
    at least a few
        or a couple

It's dark when I look
    Up the series of
        Ladders

The first ladder
    Goes up one way
The next ladder higher
    Up

Say you have a ladder
    That is on the right side
        That goes up one
            flight.

Then you have a ladder
That is on another side
    That goes up

There's a snake on
    The floor by where
        I'm standing
I look up into the
    Darkness of where
        The boy went
            There's no
Air conditioning there

I think the boy's
    Mother must not
        Have had a lot
            Of money if they
    Live up there

Something about California
    She's from California-
        She's going to California
But she's not here
    And why didn't
        She tell me when
            She's coming back
We didn't even talk
    About it

The boy goes up
    And I wait where
        The light is
            Before the series
                Of dis-jointed
        Open ladder-stairs
        Into the hot, stuffy
            Darkness starts

I figure he can go
    Get his clothes
        And come back
        Down

But it looks dangerous
    Even to climb up
        There
    -especially for a
        boy

And I just look at
    that snake as it
        writhes and moves

Say something to the
    owner of the
        house

about the snake
The owner says something like
Barely not even
    giving recognition
to the question
    Like "Oh it's just"

Like as if she can't
        even acknowledge
                the living, breathing,
                        moving snake

Like trying to mind-
        Manipulate me to
                Get my mind off whatever
                        I "didn't" see

I figure if the mother
        didn't come back by
                        the time I had
                to leave 7:30 p.m.-
                        I might have

To come up with a solution or
        Cancel the restaurant
                Job where I had to be
                        At 7:30 p.m.

You know- the restaurant
        by the forest-
                the one with a stream
                        in the somewhat
                                vicinity-
When you're walking
        away from the restaurant
                you will eventually
                        end up near a
                                stream

-And when I left with
        the boy-
to seemingly babysit him-
        or at least that's
                what I thought-

The people sitting at the
        Restaurant gave me a
                Strange, almost menacing
                Stare

The bird with the long wing span

The bird with the long wing span flies
over the water
That might make an ok photograph I
think to myself
The water's waves ripple quickly and
harshly
The water is more like a lake
Than an ocean
Yet its waves ripple quickly and harshly
To tell you the truth,
I like the ocean better
Ideally, a calm, tranquil, warm ocean

And the little girl tells us that
We have the privilege of
Sleeping underneath her
At bed time
It must be a bunk-bed of sorts
It would be nicer to have some room
To have a bed not so close to hers
Let alone have our own room

And the ground beneath is harsh
More like rocks, pebbles, stones
Than sand
It might be nice to have at least a little
sand under the feet
I don't know where he is but I feel alone
now all of a sudden
Let alone soft, warm sand
She says something about teaching us to
surf

The waves although present
Are shorter than waves in an ocean
But the water is choppy
And the water whips up and down in
short, angry chops
But it was like she would disappear
Or she was hardly there herself
Yet I knew these thoughts
That she had
I assumed they came from her